EAST CENTRAL REGIONAL LIBRARY
32050007530733
JNF 197.3 O

WITHDRAWN

Orr, Tamra.
Extreme wakeboarding

EXTREME WAKEBOARDING

TAMRA B. ORR

Cavendish
Square

New York

NOTE FROM THE PUBLISHER:
Do not attempt this sport without wearing proper safety gear and taking safety precautions.

Published in 2014 by Cavendish Square Publishing, LLC
303 Park Avenue South, Suite 1247, New York, NY 10010

Copyright © 2014 by Cavendish Square Publishing, LLC

First Edition

No part of this publication may be reproduced, stored in a retrieval system, or transmitted in any form or by any means—electronic, mechanical, photocopying, recording, or otherwise—without the prior permission of the copyright owner. Request for permission should be addressed to Permissions, Cavendish Square Publishing, 303 Park Avenue South, Suite 1247, New York, NY 10010. Tel (877) 980-4450; fax (877) 980-4454.

Website: cavendishsq.com

This publication represents the opinions and views of the author based on his or her personal experience, knowledge, and research. The information in this book serves as a general guide only. The author and publisher have used their best efforts in preparing this book and disclaim liability rising directly or indirectly from the use and application of this book.

CPSIA Compliance Information: Batch #WS13CSQ

All websites were available and accurate when this book was sent to press.

LIBRARY OF CONGRESS CATALOGING-IN-PUBLICATION DATA
Orr, Tamra.
Extreme wakeboarding / Tamra B. Orr
p. cm. — (Sports on the edge!)
Includes bibliographical references and index.
Summary: "Explores the sport of extreme wakeboarding"—Provided by publisher.
ISBN 978-1-60870-224-4 (hardcover) ISBN 978-1-62712-134-7 (paperback)
ISBN 978-1-60870-863-5 (ebook)
1. Wakeboarding—Juvenile literature. I. Title. II. Series.
GV840.W34O77 2012
797.3—dc22
2011016325

EDITOR: Christine Florie
ART DIRECTOR: Anahid Hamparian   SERIES DESIGNER: Kristen Branch

EXPERT READER: Luke Woodling, content director, *Transworld Wakeboarding*, Winter Park, Florida

Photo research by Marybeth Kavanagh

Cover photo by Michael Sohn/AP Photo
The photographs in this book are used by permission and through the courtesy of: *SuperStock*: age fotostock, 4; All Canada Photos, 23; *CORBIS*: Rick Doyle, 7, 9; Steven Georges/Press-Telegram, 10; *AP Photo*: The Charlotte Observer/Patrick Schneider, 12; Chris Polk, 35; *Getty Images*: Paul Ross Jones/Workbook, 14; Paul Kane, 19; Sam Yeh/AFP, 31; Bob Rosato/Sports Illustrated, 38; Al Tielemans/Sports Illustrated, 42; *Alamy*: TNT Magazine, 16; Dieter Wanke, 26; Tracy Ferrero, 27; Daniel Mogan, 41; *The Image Works*: Kahnert/Caro/ullstein bild, 29; *Newscom*: Mike Isler/Icon SMI 730, 32; Tim Chong/RTR, 34; Tony Donaldson/Icon SMI Icon Sports Photos, 37

Printed in the United States of America

CONTENTS

ONE
HOLD ON TIGHT!

ARE YOU READY to take on **wakes** and master jumps. Are you ready to be a wakeboarder? You aren't alone! Wakeboarding is one of the fastest-growing water sports in the world today, despite the fact that it has been around for only about twenty-five years. It got its name because the sport centers on jumping or riding a board across wakes in a body of water. It is a mix of several sports. Watch a professional wakeboarder, and you will see the

◁── WAKEBOARDING IS A SPORT THAT COMBINES THE THRILL AND ACTION OF SKATEBOARDING, SURFING, AND SNOWBOARDING—BUT ON WATER!

influence of skateboarding, surfing, snowboarding, and waterskiing. Indeed, wakeboarding came about because so many people loved all of these sports so much, they wanted to find another way to enjoy the water. All over the world, wakeboarders are testing out new moves on lakes, rivers, and oceans. If there's enough water for a boat, they are there!

CREATING A NEW SPORT

For many years people have had fun riding on water skis while being pulled behind a boat. They've learned to ride on one ski, to jump off ramps, and to ride together in teams. How could they find another way to do almost the same sport? In the mid–1980s Tony Finn, a surfer from California, came up with the answer. He developed the first board designed to be pulled behind a motorboat. He called it the Skurfer. This board was shorter and thicker than a regular surfboard and had foot straps on it. In 1990 the sports television channel ESPN showed the first Skurfer championships. Although people enjoyed watching the competition, very few were trying the sport themselves. The boards were too difficult for most people to use. It took too much skill and experience for beginners.

All of that changed when Herb O'Brien, a man who owned a water-ski company, stepped in. He took Finn's idea and made some improvements. He designed a new kind of board called the Hyperlite. It was lighter and easier to use, and had special straps known as

TONY FINN TAKES A RIDE ON HIS INVENTION, THE SKURFER.

bindings to keep the rider's feet attached to the board. This made the board safer to ride and simpler to control. It was just what the sport needed. Now everyone wanted to give wakeboarding a try.

Off to Camp!

WANT TO LEARN ALL about wakeboarding? Why not do it at camp? Across the country there are quite a few from which to choose. One is the Wakeboard Camp in Clermont, Florida. It is open year-round for girls and boys, typically ages twelve and up, as well as adults. The head coach is Kyle Schmidt, former instructional editor of *Wakeboarding* magazine. Other teachers include wakeboarders who have won Rider of the Year Awards. A week includes daily lessons, three meals a day, lodging, practice, and lots of instruction.

GETTING BETTER ALL THE TIME

As the Hyperlite was used more and more, O'Brien began changing it to make it ride even better. He made it thinner and added sharper edges to the sides so the board could cut through the water more like a ski. He added large dimples, or **phasers**, to the bottom of the board, too. This made the board easier to skim over the top of the water and made landings softer and easier to handle. It did not take long before other companies caught on to O'Brien's ideas and began making wakeboards also. Everyone kept trying to make the board a little better. Over time, the boards were made with **fins** on both ends known as **twin tips**. This made it possible for wakeboarders to ride the board in either direction.

In 1990 the World Wakeboard Association was formed. It set up the formal rules of the sport and the styles and formats that were acceptable— and which ones were not. Two years later the sport turned professional, and national competitions in wakeboarding were held. In 1993 the magazine *Wakeboarding* was launched, and interested readers were thrilled to finally be

WAKEBOARDS HAVE TWIN TIPS, WHICH ALLOW WAKEBOARDERS TO RIDE THEIR BOARDS IN BOTH DIRECTIONS.

PROFESSIONAL WAKEBOARDER JOSH SANDERS COMPETES IN THE 2005 X GAMES IN LONG BEACH, CALIFORNIA.

able to read the advice of professional riders, tips on how to do new tricks, and how to get connected with other riders. The new World Wakeboarding Championships provided international competitions for the best riders from all over the world. In 1996 the sport was added to the **X Games**, and many people got the chance to see wakeboarding for the first time.

Today wakeboarding is a hot sport that keeps drawing more and more people to it. Millions of wakeboarders all over the world spend their time out on the water, launching off a boat's wake. Think you've got what it takes to be an expert on the wakeboard? Let's find out!

TWO

BOARD, BINDINGS, AND MORE

WHEN IT COMES TO HITTING the water and having fun, it is all about the board and bindings. Before you start surfing sites and scanning stores, however, let's make sure you know the basics. For example, are you a good swimmer—a really good swimmer? If not, that is the place to start. Even though you will be wearing a life jacket or **personal flotation device (PFD)** whenever you're wakeboarding, you have to be a strong swimmer to cope with wipeouts, or **wrecks**. If your swimming skills could use some help, you can check with your school's swim coach, the local YM/YWCA, or a community recreation center that has tutors or swim teachers.

Have you had any experience with other water sports? Do you know how to water-ski or surf? The skills you have learned doing these sports will help you greatly. Of course, if you're a terrific snowboarder or skateboarder, that helps, too. Chances are you've already practiced keeping your balance, and you have personal experience on how to fall down and not get seriously hurt. If you've never done any of these sports before, however, take your time and learn slowly. Practice keeping your balance by closing your eyes and hopping—but not near anything breakable.

Are you in decent physical shape? It takes pretty strong muscles to stay up on a

MAINTAINING BALANCE ON A WAKEBOARD IS HARD WORK, BUT IT'S ONE OF THE MOST IMPORTANT SKILLS TO LEARN.

wakeboard for a long time. Some of the best riders exercise with weights regularly to make sure their muscles stay strong and flexible. Stretching your muscles before and after a ride is also a good idea. It helps you maintain flexibility, and you won't be as sore after a ride if you take the time to stretch.

Time spent on other boards may have shown you which of your feet is the dominant one. Do you put your left or your right foot in front when hopping on your skateboard or snowboard? That's the one that is dominant. If you've never done these sports, how do you know? Stand on the ground with your feet together. Have someone you trust not to take a good thing too far, push you from the back and just enough to throw you off balance. Which foot went forward first to steady you? That is most likely your dominant foot. That is the one you will put in front on almost any board you choose to ride, including a wakeboard. If it is your left foot, you are called a **regular foot** boarder. If it is your right foot, you are called a **goofy foot** rider.

THIS WAKEBOARDER IS A REGULAR FOOT BOARDER. HIS LEFT FOOT IS IN THE FORWARD POSITION ON HIS BOARD.

Choosing a Board

Typically, a wakeboard costs several hundred dollars, so you want to choose wisely. Beginning riders usually get a narrower board than the pros. Fifteen inches in width is average for young riders. The width of the board controls how quickly it turns and how easily it jumps off the water. Most boards weigh about 6 or 7 pounds and are shorter than surfboards and thicker than snowboards. Almost all boards have fins on them. Some fins are molded as part of the board, and others can be screwed in or taken off. Beginners should have two large fins on their boards because they will add stability to the rides.

A number of companies make boards specifically for new riders. The Hyperlite Motive and the O'Brien System wakeboards, for example, are especially made for newbies. These boards are more stable and allow you to learn at your own pace. Check those out online and in stores. If you have a friend with a board, look at it, too. Stand on it. Go out in the water with it. Talk to the people at the store about what kind of board to buy. Chat about it in forums online (with parental permission), and ask people's advice. Contact wakeboarding associations, and see if they have tips for buying that first board. Do your homework before you open your wallet.

One last tip: it's easy to be fooled into buying a board just because it looks great. Companies often spend a lot of money making the colors and graphics on a board look exciting rather than making the board high quality. Don't let yourself be tricked into buying an inferior board just because you like the graphics on it.

A WAKEBOARDER PREPARES FOR A RIDE BY LACING UP HIS BOOTS.

LACES AND OTHER EXTRAS

You're almost ready but still need a couple of extras. Although original wakeboarders used a type of strap to keep their ankles and feet on their boards, today most use boots with laces called bindings or with a combination of laces and Velcro straps. These attach directly to the board. When you are first beginning and will most likely fall often, you might want to use laces that release quickly as you're falling.

Boots are often expensive, running several hundred dollars, so once again you want to buy wisely. They should be snug but not tight, as they will loosen as you wear them. You might want to purchase some special **lubrication gel** for when you slide your feet into them. They can be a snug fit, and the gel can help. While some people use dishwashing soap or baby shampoo, you have to make sure the product is **water soluble** and does not contain oil. Oil puts pollution in the water. Many companies offer wakeboard packages that include the board, boots, bindings, and often a few extras. These packages can be the least expensive option for newbies.

BUYING THE EXTRAS

Once you have your board and bindings, you are almost—but not quite—ready to get started. You will also need a good helmet, a **towrope**, and a reliable PFD. Other options include a dry suit and a wet suit, depending on the climate in which you live.

A helmet is required only if you are competing or riding in a cable park, but it is always a good idea to wear one. Get one that is rated for wakeboarding, not just a simple bike helmet. Once again, ask on forums or check with your local sporting goods shop for the best type. You want to keep your head safe while out on the water, the same as you do when biking or skateboarding.

Your towrope is also quite important. It is what keeps you connected to the boat and how you will get the power and speed you need to hit the wakes and to do your tricks. You cannot use the same kind used in waterskiing. Those towropes have a lot of stretch in them and can snap backward. You need one that does not do this. The longer the rope, the higher and farther a rider can go and the more time he or she will have for doing the biggest tricks. For beginners, most experts recommend 60 feet, while professionals use 75 to 85 feet.

You absolutely must have a reliable PFD. It should be able to support your weight easily, so look to make sure for the weight the PFD is rated for. Also, if you end up with a used PFD, it should not have any worn

PREPARE WISELY BY CHOOSING A QUALITY HELMET, TOWROPE, AND PERSONAL FLOTATION DEVICE.

straps or fabric. When you put it on and get in the water, it should be strong enough to keep your head bobbing above the water easily, with no help from you. Check to make sure that the PFD has approval from the U.S. Coast Guard, as those PFDs are the only ones that come with a guarantee to keep you afloat.

If you wear glasses, you cannot wakeboard with them on. Consider buying a set of prescription goggles or wearing contact lenses. If you are going to be wakeboarding where the water stays cold year round, also consider a **neoprene** wet suit to keep you warm.

WAKEBOARDING WISE

LIKE MOST SPORTS, wakeboarding is full of jargon. Knowing the terms not only makes it easier for you to understand other wakeboarders, but also helps with videos, classes, and books. Here are some of the basic terms with which to get familiar.

AIR the amount of space between the rider and the water

BAIL to fall on your wakeboard

BOARDER a person who wakeboards, but preferred terms are *rider* or *wakeboarder*

BONK to hit an obstacle

BUTTER smooth water, also sometimes called *glass*

CHOPPY rough (as in water)

DIGGER a bad wreck

DOCK START being pulled into the water while sitting or standing on a dock

EDGES the sides of the wakeboard

FACEPLANT falling face-first into the water

FAKIE a move where you ride the board with your less dominant foot forward, also known as a *switch*

FRONT FLIP a flip forward end over end

GRABS different locations where you grasp the board; includes such names as *stalefish*, *melan*, *slob*, *crail*, and *nuclear*

OLÉ a move where you spin and then lift the board's handle over your head

SPINS rotations in the air with rider and board; includes turns from 180 to 360 degrees, plus wrapped spins in which the rider has the rope wrapped around his or her back while riding so that he or she can spin without passing the handle

STOKED excited and confident

TANTRUM a backflip over the wake

Having both a wet suit and a dry suit can make the wakeboarding season last longer, as you will stay warmer in the water despite the temperature.

FINDING HELPERS

There is one more thing to consider when starting to wakeboard. Unlike many sports, you cannot do this one alone. Most of the time you will need someone with a boat who can drive it for you—and a **spotter**. Not just any boat will work, either. It has to be a motorboat of some kind. There are boats made especially for wakeboarding. They have extra built-in tanks that can be filled with water to make them heavier. Why? This creates a bigger wake and larger waves on which you can play. If your boat does not have these tanks, you can still make it heavier by putting a cooler full of soda and snacks in it—or inviting along a few extra friends. Just make sure you don't make the boat too heavy—it is quite sinkable!

In the beginning your driver should keep the boat's speed between 14 and 18 miles per hour.

Once you've learned a bit and can do some of the advanced tricks, you can speed up. Most wakeboarding boats never go more than 24 miles per hour when pulling a rider.

The driver of the boat should have taken a safety course (some states require this), because driving for a wakeboarder is not an easy job. The driver has to maintain a steady speed and avoid making any big

WHEN WAKEBOARDING, MAKE SURE AN EXPERIENCED BOATER AND SPOTTER ACCOMPANY YOU.

changes. He or she has to know when to speed up or slow down. The spotter's job is to keep an eye on the rider at all times and to watch for trouble or for a message from the wakeboarder.

Typically you use hand signals to communicate with your spotter. Why can't you just yell at each other? No one would be able to hear over the boat engine.

Instead, you have to learn basic signals such as thumbs-up for "faster," thumbs-down for "slower," a wave for "I'm okay," and a pat on your head for "I'm done now." Hand signals can vary from one spotter or rider to another, so make sure that you and your spotter understand the same signals. The spotter may send a message to the rider also, such as "There is a wake up ahead" or "We are turning around." A misunderstanding while you're boarding can be dangerous.

Now that you know what equipment you need, it's time to learn a few tricks. Ready to hit those waves? Let's go!

THREE

TIME FOR TRICKS

YOU'VE FOUND YOUR equipment, a boat, a driver, and a spotter. You've been practicing your balance and swimming skills, and you know which foot is your dominant one. You are ready to get wet!

Proper Positioning

The first thing to practice is simply getting up and out of the water on your board. If you've been waterskiing, this may be simple. However, if you haven't, just getting started can feel strange and take some time to learn. Go out into deep water. Face your body and your board toward the boat. Your knees should be bent with your feet pointing toward the front end of your board. Hold on to the towrope with your knuckles on top and your arms over your knees.

Signal the spotter when you are ready to start going forward. As the boat moves, you will feel a tug on the rope. Let the boat pull you up, and stick out your chest (not your butt!). Stay crouched until the board starts to **plane**, or skim the surface of the water. Slowly extend your legs to a standing position. If you stand up too soon, you will most likely fall.

THIS WAKEBOARDER IS IN THE CROUCHED POSITION BEFORE SHE EXTENDS HER LEGS TO STAND.

Finally, turn the board so that your hips and shoulders are in line with the boat.

As you stand up, keep your arms out and slightly bend your elbows. If you tuck in the rope against your stomach, you will most likely fall facedown in the water. If you lean back on your board just a little, you will increase the force between your board and the water. Remember to keep your pelvis and eyes pointed toward either the boat or the skyline. The tip in wakeboarding is, where the hips go, the board goes. Look too far up or down and you will have an out-of-control board. While standing, about 70 percent of your weight should be on your back foot. As you learn to gain more control, you will balance between the front and back feet, but for now, this will keep you up longer.

Once you are up, practice getting comfortable riding behind the boat. Have your driver run you through a number of starts until it begins to feel more natural.

PRACTICE RIDING BEHIND A BOAT BEFORE YOU TRY OUT SOME TRICKS.

Going Extreme

You may just want to ride behind a boat for some days or weeks until you are comfortable enough to try learning a few tricks. Since the key is having fun, that is just fine! If you do decide you want to stretch your boundaries and get a little more extreme, here are a couple of the easiest tricks to learn.

Start off by getting comfortable holding on to the towrope with just one hand. See how you have to shift your balance to compensate for it.

There are two kinds of tricks to do on a wakeboard. The first one is surface tricks. You do these without leaving the surface of the water. The others are wakeboarding tricks in which you usually catch some air. After all, that is really what wakeboarding is all about!

One of the most basic surface tricks is the **fakie**, or switchstance. As its name suggests, it just means switching your feet—putting the nondominant one in front. Learning to do this will make doing more complicated tricks later much easier.

Once you have a little more skill, try a surface 180. In this trick, regular foot boarders go left and goofy foot riders go right. You are switching from one side to the other. In the surface 360 you let go with one hand, turn your back to the boat, reach behind you and grab the rope to make a full circle. If you pass the rope over your head instead of behind your back, it is called an olé!

THIS WAKEBOARDER PERFORMS A SURFACE 360.

HERE ARE SOME of the most common tricks for newbies to learn, in order of easiest to hardest:

- Stand up on the board for five seconds
- Ride with one hand on the handle for five seconds
- Cross one wake
- Cross both wakes
- Wave to the boat judge
- Crouch down and touch the water
- Get in the air off the wake
- Surface 180 (board changes direction from back to front or front to back)
- Sideslide (board carves the wake like a surfer would carve a wave)
- Surface 360 (board rotates 360 degrees on the surface of the water)

RIDING THE WAKE

What about the nonsurface tricks? They are the ones that use wakes. A wake is simply the two waves of displaced water that is pushed behind a boat. You can use these strong waves to jump off and do other tricks. Of course, not just any wake will work. Experts say that if a wake has too much curl at the top, it is too mushy. If it's too straight, it is too hard.

Crossing a wake takes skill and practice—but it is worth the rush of feeling it under you, lifting you up! Approach it with your knees bent. Go slowly. If you go too fast you will have to pull up your legs quickly. You can also choose to jump the wake instead of crossing it. In this case you should stand tall, with your knees slightly bent. You will find yourself propelled up in the air!

Want to ramp up these tricks? Add in a few grabs. Squat down and grab the front or back of your board like skateboarders do when up in the air. You can also grab the sides. Stick out your leg

A WAKEBOARDER GRABS THE SIDE OF HER BOARD AS SHE CATCHES AIR!

THE TANTRUM IS A TRULY EXTREME TRICK! IT'S A BACKFLIP OFF A WAKE.

when you're doing it, and it becomes a tailbone (rear leg) or nosebone (front leg) grab.

If you watch the pros you can see that they take all of these moves to a whole new level. They perform all kinds of flips and tricks. They do moves such as the tantrum—which is a full backflip off the wake. Or they do more than 180s or 360s—they do 540s (a spin and a half) or even 720s (two full spins). There are some who attempt to do four—or more—full spins!

In recent years some athletes have taken wakeboarding a step further—to **wakeskating**. These boards look like fat skateboards with fins where there would usually be wheels. Riders do not have bindings; they prefer to wear special shoes that let water drain out the sides.

WAKEBOARD HEROES

OVER THE YEARS there have been many amazing wakeboarders. Wakeboarding is a sport that tends to attract young people, and competitors are often in their late teens or early twenties. Some of the most famous faces in wakeboarding are Phillip Soven, Danny Harf, Parks Bonifay, and Dallas Friday.

Meet Phillip and Danny

Twenty-two-year-old Phillip Soven grew up in Windermere, Florida, and learned to wakeboard on Lake Spear. He was undefeated in the 2008 Pro Tour.

His favorite stance is goofy at 12 degrees. Along with wakeboarding, he loves to snowboard and do motocross.

Growing up with friends who lived on a lake helped Danny Harf to become a fan of water sports. From the first day he spotted a Skurferboard and gave it a try, he knew what he wanted to do. Recently, he nailed an amazing 1260—three and a half turns! "People will go above and beyond that," he said in an interview with *Wakeboarding* magazine. "The sport will just keep growing. There will always be something new to do. . . . Any time you land something new, you get that

PHILLIP SOVEN COMPETES IN THE MEN'S SEMIFINALS IN THE 2007 WAKEBOARD WORLD CUP IN SINGAPORE.

adrenaline rush. That inspires me to keep pushing it and make it happen."

STARTING YOUNG

Parks Bonifay won his very first world record when he became the youngest person ever to put on a pair of water skis. He was six months old! Since then he has become one of the world's most famous wakeboarders. He won events at the X Games when he was only fourteen and is known for trying anything—including boarding off icebergs off the coast of Canada. In an interview with

DANNY HARF HOLDS HIS GOLD MEDAL AFTER WINNING AT THE 2003 X GAMES IN LONG BEACH, CALIFORNIA.

Wakeboarding magazine, he said, "I guess I've always tried to go for it as hard as I can, and push the limits of what I could do. Besides that, I've always tried to explore different aspects of wakeboarding . . . anything

35

From Rider to Designer

OVER THE LAST two decades Greg Nelson has been an important part of wakeboarding in almost every possible way. He started waterskiing when he was little and his grandmother bought him a board. He put water-ski fins on it, and it wasn't long before he was wakeboarding and snowboarding every chance he had. "It was snowboarding . . . that inspired my riding early on," he said in an interview with Fuel TV. "I watched every snowboard film I could get my hands on and tried to emulate that on the water."

· Nelson founded his own company, Double UP Wakeboards, and designed his own equipment. His was the first rider-owned and -operated wakeboard company. In this role, Nelson has promoted, filmed, and coached the sport. It came as little surprise when he was included in the list of 8 Most Influential Wakeboarders Ever. Today he is marketing manager for Hyperlite Wakeboards. Nelson's wife, Evelyn, is a former coach and instructor for competitive wakeboarding also. Together they run the Nelson Premier Wakeboard Clinics.

IN 2002 PARKS BONIFAY COMPETED IN THE X GAMES IN PHILADELPHIA, PENNSYLVANIA.

that's different and hasn't been done. I just try to keep it moving."

NOT FOR BOYS ONLY

Don't be fooled into thinking that only guys go into wakeboarding. One of the most amazing players in the whole sport is a woman named Dallas Friday. At twenty-four years old, she has already won every possible award in the sport, including the Best Female

AT THE AGE OF FOURTEEN, DALLAS FRIDAY WON AT THE GRAVITY GAMES. THAT SAME YEAR SHE WON THE WORLD CUP.

Action Sports Athlete in 2004, Queen of Wake and Wakeboard World Games Champion, and World Cup Champion. She won events at the X Games and the Gravity Games when she was only fourteen years old!

Friday was the first woman to do several complicated tricks in competition. According to Friday, she got started in wakeboarding because her brother enjoyed it. He took her out one day, and she loved it. "I was hooked from that day forward and never looked back to gymnastics," she says. "I found a sport I loved and was destined to do."

Who will be tomorrow's wakeboard hero? Who knows? Since the national and international competitions always include quite a few teens, maybe the next star will be you!

FIVE

THE FUTURE OF WAKEBOARDING

IT IS HARD TO GUESS where wakeboarding will go next. As boards change, boats get more high-tech and riders get more and more daring. No one is sure what will happen at the next local, national, or international competition. One of the biggest changes to come along since the sport started, however, was the creation of cable parks, or parks that make it so that you don't need a boat or a driver to take a ride on the water.

No Boat Necessary

Certainly an aspect of wakeboarding that made it possible—or impossible—to do was finding someone who had a boat and was willing to use it to pull you whenever you wanted to hit the water. To change that, more than 140 parks have sprung up all over the world to take the boat out of wakeboarding. Currently, most of them are found in Europe, Africa, Asia, and Australia, but they are being built throughout the United States as well.

Cable parks are built so that each rider is pulled through the water and over ramps by a large cable in the air rather than by a boat of any kind. A series of towers surrounding the waterway connects the towrope so that the riders have a long and smooth ride. The cable rides slightly higher than a regular towrope, which allows riders to use another approach to their tricks.

How can riders jump a wake if there is no boat to create one? Good question. Generally, they create tension with the cable and then release it, which sends them up in the air. Riders also hit kickers, or ramps, to send them up into the sky.

How do they take off if there is no boat to pull them up out of

A WAKEBOARDER IS PULLED BY A CABLE AT THE ROTHER VALLEY COUNTRY PARK IN SHEFFIELD, ENGLAND.

SLIDER PARKS—ABOVE AND BELOW

SOME OF THE MOST advanced wakeboarders like to head out to slider parks to practice their tricks. These parks are a little like skate parks, only, instead of being made of concrete, they are made out of wood and plastic and are located on the water. Ramps, slides, rails, and other obstacles are anchored on the surface, and boarders use them to learn and perfect their moves. Some of the most extreme riders have taken the idea a step further and have created underground slider parks inside caves. Using cables, they jump, twist, turn, and splash down in relative darkness many feet under the ground.

THERE'S A GOOD REASON WHY WAKEBOARDING HAS BECOME ONE OF THE MOST EXCITING SPORTS. GIVE IT A TRY!

the water? Riders stand on a deck with one end of the cable in their hands. At the same time, the other end is attached to a carrier. The carrier pulls the riders right off the deck and straight into the water.

In the Media

Since 2001 there have been international cable wakeboard competitions. In 2005 wakeboarding was included in the World Games and was featured on television. Millions of people tuned in to watch, and a new passion for a favorite sport was born. Each year the interest in the sport keeps climbing. More and more people are finding a board, putting on their bindings, and slamming across the water surface in search of new highs, new thrills, and new tricks. Ready to join them?

GLOSSARY

bindings laces that keep your ankles and boots attached to a wakeboard

fakie a trick in which you ride the board with your nondominant foot forward

fins permanent or movable pieces on a wakeboard that help with direction

goofy foot a person whose right foot is dominant

lubrication gel a substance that lets a foot slip into a boot more easily

neoprene a synthetic rubber that is resistant to oils

personal flotation device (PFD) a life jacket or device that keeps a person afloat

phasers dimples or depressions on the bottom of a wakeboard

plane to skim the surface of the water

regular foot a person whose left foot is dominant

spotter the person in the boat who is responsible for watching the wakeboarder for signals, possible problems, and so on

towrope the rope that connects a wakeboarder to the boat

twin tips tips on the front and back of a wakeboard

wakes the tracks of waves left by an object moving through water

wakeskating wakeboarding on a smaller board without bindings

water soluble able to dissolve easily in water

wrecks wipeouts on a wakeboard

X Games an annual competition featuring extreme-action sports

FIND OUT MORE

BOOKS

Boese, Kristin, and Christian Spreckels. *Kitesurfing: The Complete Guide*. New York: Wiley, 2008.

Favret, Ben. *Water Skiing and Wakeboarding*. Champaign, IL: Human Kinetics, 2010.

Otfinoski, Steven. *Extreme Skateboarding*. New York: Cavendish Square Publishing, LLC, 2014.

DVDs

Canvas, VAS Entertainment, 2009.

Out of the Pond, Billabong, 2009.

Transgression, Gator Boards, 2007.

WEBSITES

TransWorld Wakeboarding Magazine

http://wakeboardingmag.com/

This website features everything from the most popular wakeboarding videos to photo galleries of top riders and articles on technique.

USA Wakeboard

www.usawakeboard.com/

This organization is part of USA Waterski, currently the world's largest water-ski federation, and offers membership. It features a separate section for wakeboarding and posts information on national competitions.

Waterski Magazine

http://waterskimag.com/

This online site advertises the bimonthly magazine *Waterski* and includes photos, forums, schools, and an e-newsletter.

World Wakeboard Association

www.thewwa.com/

The headquarters for the World Wakeboard Association, this site offers news about upcoming competitions, shows current videos, and features the blogs of six of the best-known U.S. wakeboarders.

INDEX

Page numbers in **boldface** are illustrations

ABOUT THE AUTHOR

TAMRA ORR is the author of more than 250 books for readers of all ages. A graduate of Ball State University, Orr has a degree in secondary education and English and has written thousands of national and state assessment questions. Currently, she lives in the Pacific Northwest with her dog, cat, husband, and three teenagers. In her fourteen spare minutes each day, she loves to read, write letters, and travel around the state of Oregon, marveling at the breathtaking scenery.